CW01667329

Amgueddfa Genedlaethol Cymru
National Museum of Wales
Cardiff 1980

Alan Sorrell: Early Wales Re-created

This book is published on the occasion of the opening of an exhibition of watercolour reconstructions of Welsh ancient monuments by the late Alan Sorrell in the collections of the National Museum of Wales, Lady Fox and the Ancient Monuments Branch of the Welsh Office organised by D.W. Dykes, Secretary of the National Museum

ISBN 0 7200 0228 1

Acknowledgements

I would like to express my deep appreciation to Mrs. Elizabeth Sorrell for her invaluable assistance in the preparation of the exhibition and this book and for so readily making available to me examples of her late husband's work and other material. My thanks are due also to Dr. Arnold Taylor, Professor Henry Loyn, Professor W. F. Grimes and especially to Lady Fox for their help.

I am grateful to Professor Sir Idris Foster, Chairman of the Ancient Monuments Board for Wales for writing the Preface; to Mr. Peter Humphries of the Ancient Monuments Branch of the Welsh Office for contributing the introductory section on 'Alan Sorrell and Ancient Monuments in Wales' in collaboration with the writer and for his compilation of the catalogue entries in consultation with members of the Department of Archaeology of the National Museum and the writer; and to Dr. Michael Thompson, head of the Ancient Monuments Branch of the Welsh Office and 'joint begetter' of the exhibition, without whose help and support it would not have been possible.

Grateful acknowledgement is also made to the following: Aerofilms and Aero Pictorial Limited: p. 64; Director in Aerial Photography, University of Cambridge: p. 26; Lady Fox: pp. 17 51; Illustrated London News and Sketch Limited: pp. 6 10 (bottom right); Photoflight Limited: pp. 30 32; The President and Fellows, Magdalen College, Oxford: p.12; A Private Collector: p. 10 (bottom left); Royal Commission on Ancient and Historical Monuments in Wales: p. 46; Royal Commission on Historical Monuments (England): p. 66; Mrs. Elizabeth Sorrell and Mr. G. A. Tanner: p. 3; Mrs. Elizabeth Sorrell: p. 10 (top left) 21; Southend-on-Sea Borough Council (Beecroft Art Gallery, Westcliff-on-Sea): p.4; H. Tempest (Cardiff) Limited: p. 34; Mr. F.D Todman: p. 10 (top right); Trustees of the Imperial War Museum: pp. 7 8; Warwickshire Education Authority: p. 9; West Air Photography: pp. 28 38.

D.W.D.

Preface

It gives me much pleasure to write a brief preface to this book which is published on the occasion of the opening of the exhibition *Alan Sorrell: Early Wales Re-created.*

The idea of an exhibition arose during a conversation in 1977 between Dr. Michael Thompson, head of the Ancient Monuments Branch of the Welsh Office and Mr. D. W. Dykes, Secretary of the National Museum of Wales. They thought that an exhibition of the watercolours by Alan Sorrell in the collections of the Ancient Monuments Branch and the National Museum would be a fitting memorial to the artist who died in 1974. The combination of photographs of what actually survives of the monuments and the original paintings will give us some idea of how much research and imagination had to be used in making the drawings.

As Mr. Dykes points out in his Introduction, and as we can see from the selection of his work which has been illustrated, Sorrell was both an artist of wide compass and a master of a variety of media. It is, however, as an outstanding 'reconstruction' artist that Sorrell is best known and it is to this aspect of his work, and in particular to his associations with Wales, that the exhibition and this book are devoted.

By his insistence on the accuracy of the details of his drawings and watercolours doubtless Sorrell gave a further stimulus to archaeologists to think carefully about the appearance of the buildings that they were excavating. At the same time the verve and vivacity of his work has created a lively and enlightened interest in early Britain, especially among young people. How great a loss to the important work of extending popular knowledge of archaeology and history was Sorrell's death six years ago may be gauged from the remarkable pictures which we can continue to admire in the pages of this catalogue.

Idris Foster
Chairman, Ancient Monuments Board for Wales

A biographical note

Born in London, February 1904
Associate Royal College of Art, 1924–28
Prix de Rome for Mural Painting, 1928
British School at Rome, 1928–1931
Instructor in Drawing at the Royal College of Art, 1931–1948
War Service with the Royal Air Force and Air Ministry, 1941–45
Associate of the Royal Watercolour Society, 1937
Member of the Royal Watercolour Society, 1941
Died, December 1974.

Works in permanent collections

The Tate Gallery, the Imperial War Museum, the National Museum of Wales, the Ashmolean Museum, the Rhodes Memorial Museum, the Museum of London, various provincial museums and the collections of the Ancient Monuments Branches of the Department of the Environment, the Scottish Office and the Welsh Office.

Alan Sorrell: mirror image self portrait, 1972

Introduction

Alan Sorrell has been described as the 'Last of the line of "history" painters in the eighteenth century sense'. This description, while it pays tribute to Sorrell's power as an imaginative narrative artist, is perhaps a shade facile and incomplete. It does not do proper justice to the wide compass of his work, his versatility and his individual style, nor does it sufficiently recognise his artistic roots. 'I would die artistically', he once said, 'if I could not work in more than one direction'. A master of a variety of media, oils, watercolour and gouache, he ranged freely over portraiture, mural paintings, topographical and industrial drawings and, from his earliest student days commercial art. Landscape and figure subjects were his true love and real penchant, themes to which he constantly returned and which he was to develop in the remarkable murals he completed in the nineteen-forties and fifties.

Very much heir to the pre-Impressionist tradition of European visual art Sorrell was a Romantic with a free-ranging imagination and almost Gothick predilection for the dramatic. At the same time, however, he was a punctilious practitioner of the classical principles of drawing and the possessor of a sharp and insistent eye for veracious detail. To Sorrell the *subject* was always the *sine qua non*, but the essence of his interpretation was personal. At no time, therefore, can he be dismissed as a mere narrative illustrator or sterile recorder of actuality, even 'imagined actuality', since a factual recording was to him convincing only when it was seen through the personality of the artist himself and recreated with conviction. Sorrell's happy binding together of the two strands of the accuracy of the draughtsman and recorder and the imagination of the artist is the reason why so much of his work is attractive to the beholder. This, and the deceptively easy technique he developed in his earliest murals of using a high eye-level to enable him to distribute numbers of animated groups of figures over the greater part of the picture surface and to take the utmost advantage of his love of incident, constantly grip the viewer's attention and give life to his pictures. His feel for

The mural 'Blake's refit at Leigh' at the Central Library, Southend-on-Sea, 1932

landscape, too, even when so often the result may appear sombre or even bleak, allowed him to create an arresting atmosphere that pervaded his direct subject.

The apparently effortless combination of draughtsmanship, technique and artistry saw its fulfilment in his imaginative historical 'reconstructions', a creative art for which he is best known to the public and which, therefore, in the popular mind so masks his other work. For years, throughout the nineteen-fifties and sixties whenever a graphic interpretation of an historical event or place was needed for a publication or television it was to Sorrell that one turned to be sure that the reconstruction would be both academically plausible and stimulating to the public mind. In one sense it is to Sorrell's development of this particular genre that the present exhibition is devoted.

Sorrell's family roots lay in remotest rural Essex where his forebears had lived for many generations. His rural ancestry had a wholesome fascination for him and it is hardly surprising, therefore, that much of his best work, in theme, technique and vision reflects an elemental way of life close to nature and to the soil. It was, perhaps, also this association in his mind with a distant rural past that explains his natural taste and talent for archaeological and historical subjects.

Sorrell was born in London on 11 February 1904, the son of Ernest Sorrell, a skilled master-jeweller whose own father had moved from Essex in the latter part of the nineteenth century. At the age of ten he was sent to school at Leigh-on-Sea and then went on to a commercial school. It was not long, however, before he began training for his true vocation at the Southend School of Art and after a period as a letterer and designer he entered the Royal College of Art at the age of twenty in 1924. The quality of his work and his enthusiasm and integrity of character soon attracted the attention of Sir William Rothenstein who was Principal of the College at the time. In 1928 Sorrell was awarded the Prix de Rome for mural painting and spent the next three years at the British School at Rome.

This period of study in Italy had a decisive and lasting effect on his work. It was here that he derived his fascination for Roman history and through his contact with archaeologists and historians at the School developed an understanding of their approach to their disciplines. One of his fellow students was Aileen Henderson an archaeologist who later, as Lady Fox, was to introduce Sorrell to her husband, Sir Cyril Fox, and the National Museum of Wales. Lady Fox remembers Sorrell 'as a dark thin young man with a stammer, diffident yet determined. Like the other artists there, he affected to dislike the Roman scene and to despise the Forum and other monuments, yet it is clear that, whether consciously or unconciously, he absorbed the Roman idiom which was the basis and strength of his later work'.

In these years too he travelled extensively through Europe and Scandinavia and on his return to London in 1931 he was invited by Rothenstein to join the staff of the Royal College of Art as an instructor of drawing. In that year he began a major four-year commission of a series of murals depicting events in local history for the Central Library at Southend-on-Sea. Besides being an important landmark in his career the work also enabled him to develop techniques that he was later to apply with conspicuous success to other forms. In 1936 Sorrell visited Iceland, the stark character of which made a special appeal to him and inspired some thirty watercolours which were shown at his first one-man exhibition at the Walker Gallery in London in 1937. His taste for the dramatic, which pervades all his work, was amply illustrated in these paintings and equally so in his first ventures into archaeological reconstruction which he also began in 1936.

The combination of art and historical reconstruction began almost by chance. The excavation of Roman remains at Leicester in 1936 by the late Dame Kathleen Kenyon aroused Sorrell's interest but purely in a visual sense. He made some sketches which were shown to the then editor of the *Illustrated London News*, the late Sir Bruce Ingram, himself a connoisseur of Old Master drawings. Ingram accepted the sketches and further suggested that a reconstruction drawing by Sorrell, of the building, then thought

Sketch of the excavations at Leicester, 1936

Sorrell's earliest reconstruction drawing of the 'Basilica' at Leicester, 1936

to be a basilica should be reproduced by the magazine. Ingram's underlying idea was not to attempt the impossibility of constructing for the reader any exact reproduction of the basilica but rather to aim for a picture of probability: to convey to the reader from the bare ruins what the archaeologist could see in his mind's eye. The success of this work led directly to Sorrell's commissioning by the National Museum of Wales to prepare reconstructions of the Roman town at Caerwent and the legionary fortress at Caerleon and also to drawings for other museums and archaeologists such as those of Maiden Castle for the late Sir Mortimer Wheeler. Sorrell had established the respectability of 'reconstruction drawing' – a term he always disliked – and was fast becoming its foremost practitioner in the country.

The outbreak of the Second World War, however, interrupted Sorrell's increasing output – his work for the Royal College of Art, on murals, archaeological reconstructions and on posters for the G.P.O. and the London Passenger Transport Board. Sorrell enlisted in the Royal Air Force but in 1941 he was transferred to the Air Ministry to become a camouflage officer. In the same year he was elected a member of the Royal Watercolour Society. His wartime experiences he recorded in a series of drawings and paintings and particularly vivid are some dramatic night scenes of the hard winter of 1941.

The War ended, Sorrell returned to his work as a watercolourist and a mural painter executing several fine imaginary panels for a number of commissions including 'The Seasons', a remarkable scheme of technical and thematic difficulty for the Oken Secondary Modern School at Warwick, and a series of drawings of Hinkley Point Power Station.

In 1947 Sorrell married Elizabeth Tanner, a fine watercolourist and mural painter of great originality. They converted a former 'Peculiar People's' Chapel in Thundersley, near Benfleet in Essex, into the ideal home and studio for two working artists and enjoyed a particularly happy family life there with their three children, all now artists themselves. For Sorrell it was a return to his roots and

Recruits leaving camp – a wartime drawing of life in the R.A.F., 1941

'Airman's billet' – a wartime drawing of life in the R.A.F., 1944

his happy marriage gave him the necessary security for his work. Elizabeth Sorrell's own work is based firmly in the traditions of the English School of Watercolourists. With her interests stretching back to medieval art and so much of her inspiration lying in the fields and gardens of Essex she was the perfect partner to sustain and encourage her husband.

Sorrell became much involved in the Festival of Britain and matched his ability to create imaginary landscapes and architecture there with his reconstructions of Jericho, the Palace of Minos at Knossos and Mohenjo-Daro in the Dome of Discovery. The fifties saw Sorrell's energies becoming increasingly directed to reconstruction painting and drawing. He was employed as a special artist for the *Illustrated London News*, collaborated closely with the late Sir Ian Richmond on reconstructions of Roman sites in the north of England, and began his association with the Ministry of Works with drawings of Jarlshof, the site of a Viking farming community in the Shetlands, and of subjects connected with Hadrian's Wall. His earlier connection with the National Museum of Wales was taken up again and a series of reconstructions of Roman London was commissioned by the Director of the London Museum, Professor W. F. Grimes, who was, at the time, carrying out the exciting post-war excavations of Roman and medieval London. Sorrell, whom Professor Grimes had known since the early Cardiff days, was a natural choice for panoramas of the developing Roman city, drawings of individual sites and dramatic scenes within the Walbrook Mithraeum. Other archaeological work on Roman and medieval Britain, historical drawings for books, aimed particularly at the young, and reconstructions for television followed. Sorrell was soon established as the reconstruction artist *par excellence* and his activity in this genre began to dominate his work. Whenever an historical reconstruction was needed Sorrell was the person approached.

Always a keen traveller and anxious to seek out the past, Sorrell went to Greece and Turkey in 1954 for the *Illustrated London News*. From this journey resulted a large number of 'on the spot'

Part of the decoration 'The Seasons' at Warwick Oken Secondary Modern School

'Penmaen Castle beseiged'. A drawing for Norman Britain *by Henry Loyn and Alan Sorrell, 1966*

Inside the Queen's Temple, Abu Simbel, 1962

Agamemnon's Homecoming

Hinkley Point Power Station, 1964

drawings of Athens. Mycenae and Istanbul. Sorrell also made reconstructions of the Agora in Athens (in conjunction with Professor Homer Thompson) and of other classical sites and a fine imaginative picture of 'Agamemnon's Homecoming' showing the Lion Gate at Mycenae.

In 1962 at the request of Ingram Sorrell was commissioned to record for the *Illustrated London News* the monuments and places which were to be flooded by the building of the Aswan High Dam on the Nile. In the resulting drawings of Nubia Sorrell duly recorded the scenes required of him but such was his artistry that he was able to go beyond the purely visual account to create an atmosphere not only conveying the actuality of the present but redolent of the ancient past.

It was his ability to depict a scene – to set his subject in a peopled landscape that gave scale and actuality – and at the same time to conjure up an atmosphere implying a past and a future, however daunting that might be, that made Sorrell such an outstanding artist. Sorrell once defined archaeology as the study of people in their environment.

> *'When we accept this concept of archaeology then buildings can take their place, literally in the picture. No longer shall we be expected to tolerate the dumpy little figures which are supposed to "give scale" to their surroundings: rather must the actors in the comedy or drama be actively engaged, walking along streets, defending fortifications, worshipping in temples and so on. They will be enveloped in atmosphere, under the moving sky: sheltering from a rainstorm or buffeted by the wind, and the artist will convince us that the ugly little stubs of wall (all too carefully tidied up) which are so often preserved as the final achievement of the archaeologist are merely indications of what were once upon a time the dwelling places of people very much like ourselves'.*

Sorrell saw each scene he painted as a living continuum and it was his facility in communicating 'life' while at the same time scrupulously conveying the interpretation of the archaeologist or historian that so captured the public's imagination. Obviously he had his differences with the experts when they felt they had to avoid being definite where evidence was slender. He would always defer to the specialist, however, while still aiming at a vigorous re-creation. When he completed his drawing of the Roman fort at The Lunt near Coventry, for example, the interpretation of some of the buildings was uncertain so he showed them in course of construction.

> *'My approach involved thinking of history as a continuous process. People are alive and active round us now; they were just as alive and active round others in past times. Then, as I am an artist first of all, shapes and forms are important to me. So I try to see things as they were and build up interesting pictures. Strong imagination helps to define subjects clearly'.*

Sorrell's tragic death in 1974 was a sad loss to both art and archaeology which he had done so much to bring together. Views change in the light of archaeological revisionism, but Sorrell's paintings and drawings will remain as inspired works of art which in their time conveyed to the public in vivid form the latest archaeological interpretation. Archaeology must always be deeply indebted to the artist. Through his work he made the specialists think about the appearance of the buildings they were excavating, he spread knowledge, he aroused interest and brought the subject alive in the eyes of the public.

D. W. Dykes

The Senior Common Room at Magdalen College, Oxford. Winter, 1954

Alan Sorrell and the National Museum of Wales

Alan Sorrell's connection with the National Museum of Wales went back, as we have seen, to the nineteen-thirties. His sketches and reconstruction drawing of the recently discovered Roman buildings at Leicester for Bruce Ingram and the *Illustrated London News* had made a considerable impact upon the archaeological world. These illustrations had been seen by Sir Cyril Fox, then Director of the National Museum, and a distinguished archaeologist whose wife had known Sorrell as a fellow student at the British School at Rome in the twenties. Their publication came at an opportune moment since V. E. Nash-Williams, the Museum's Keeper of Archaeology, was at the time engaged in the excavation of the legionary fortress at Caerleon. Both Nash-Williams and Fox had felt for some years that models or illustrations to give the layman some likely notion of what Roman ruins (here or at the nearby Romano-British town of Caerwent, *Venta Silurum*, two-thirds of which had long been excavated) would have been in their heyday were essential in the Museum's presentation of such excavations to the public.

Nash-Williams's interest was in the civic side of Roman life and it was agreed that Sorrell-type drawings of Caerwent combining as accurate as possible reconstruction of buildings with the verve of the bustling activity of the town would make the greater informed appeal to the public in the first instance.

Lady Fox suggested that Sorrell himself might be willing to carry out the work and he was invited to Cardiff for preliminary discussions. Lady Fox recalls that he first came to Cardiff in the Spring of 1937.

> *'It was May when he came and I took him for a walk up the Wenallt in the flush of new green leaves, bluebells and spring flowers. When I exclaimed on its beauty, he said he didn't really like it, it was too green, like lettuces, and he preferred more sombre tones. This is very evident in all his paintings with their strong dark skies and windswept landscape and was part of his perpetual attitude to life'.*

On the basis of Sorrell's Leicester drawings for the *Illustrated London News* – which had been done in black and white 'body colour', strengthened with chalk and ink – and his colour drawing of a contemporary Icelandic farm (later acquired for the Museum through the generosity of the late Sir Leonard Twiston-Davies), the Museum decided to commission Sorrell to produce three colour drawings depicting Roman Caerwent, one large general view (**9**) and two smaller illustrations: a house surrounding a courtyard (**13**) and a building thought at the time to be a church opposite the forum (**14**). Sorrell suggested that

> *'As the purpose of these pictures is to bring the historic scene in all its familiar surroundings before the Museum visitor with the maximum of vividness I consider a treatment in colour (rather like that of the Icelandic watercolour. . . . .) would be suitable, since by presenting a place or incident in this manner it is possible to express the forms very clearly and to suggest at the same time a certain exciting dramatic note which I believe would be a highly desirable quality in these reconstructions'.*

Sorrell expressed the hope of being able to show that an historical reconstruction could also be a work of art and so have a 'far greater power of education and attraction than a possibly accurate drawing where form and design have perhaps not received such particular attention'.

The next few months were taken up in visits to Caerwent to assimilate its topography and to choose viewpoints that would allow the creation of imaginative scenes but at the same time show only the more certain elements of the site. A sensitive appreciation, too, of the buildings to be depicted and their historical and social setting was required so that much time was spent in the study of source material both at the Museum in Cardiff, and in London and Rome. The preparation of Sorrell's preliminary sketches involved the detailed co-operation of both

An Icelandic Farm, 1936

the Foxes and Nash-Williams in trying to resolve a number of tricky issues such as the existence and most plausible form of Roman chimneys, and Professor Grimes remembers how searching Sorrell's questions could be in his pursuit of accuracy and how insistent he always was on getting details as near to the truth as possible.

Sorrell's method of drawing was unique. Having first established in his mind his composition by making a thumb-nail sketch he would then begin on the final paper by roughing in with charcoal. In this way he fixed his main shapes. On top of this preliminary plan he would then work with a mixture of media using pastel, chalk, conté, watercolour and inks as he felt the need. His preliminary sketches he would send to the experts with marginal notes and queries for comment and in the light of their replies build up to his final drawing.

Sorrell's panorama of Caerwent was submitted to the Museum in November 1937 and the two smaller pictures the following year. The paintings were received with enthusiasm and Nash-Williams was to say in his Annual Report for 1937/38

> *'combining artistic insight with accuracy of archaeological detail, the reconstructions give a vivid impression of life in Roman Britain and offer a new technique of presentation which it is hoped to extend to other important archaeological sites'.*

Fox and Nash-Williams were delighted with the finished drawings which had owed so much to their collaboration and to the readiness and precision with which Sorrell had incorporated their ideas. The Museum Council was also enthusiatic and immediately commissioned Sorrell to undertake three more watercolour drawings illustrating the legionary fortress at Caerleon. The Council also agreed to the original Caerwent drawings being reproduced in the *Illustrated London News* and splendid spreads of these with commentaries by Nash-Williams appeared in the magazine on 15 October 1938 and 18 March 1939. The Caerleon watercolours – a panorama of the fortress (**4**) and views of barrack buildings (**6**) and of the amphitheatre (**5**) – were completed in 1939, but owing to the exigencies of the War they did not appear in the magazine in monochrome until 8 April 1944, again with a commentary by Nash-Williams. Sorrell thought – no doubt with his R.A.F. experience in mind – that the panorama was particularly appropriate for reproduction because of its topical similarity with military camps of the Second World War.

The success of the first six watercolours persuaded Fox that a further series should be undertaken, but both he and Nash-Williams considered that, at least for the time being, the importance of Roman Wales had been exhausted. Fox, therefore, suggested that Sorrell should turn his attention to the field of pre-history. He thought that a drawing of a chambered tomb 'would be a very fine thing' and that a round barrow should be 'a fit subject for your scholarly and imaginative pen. Thirdly Nash-Williams has investigated one of our great hill-forts – Llanmelin. I can imagine nothing more exciting than a drawing of such'.

By the end of 1940, again with the detailed help of Fox, Sorrell had completed his three drawings of the interment at the Tinkinswood Neolithic Long Cairn (**1**), the sacrificial offering of the corn sheaf at Pond Cairn, Coity (Bronze Age) (**2**) and a scene at the entrance of Llanmelin Early Iron Age hill-fort (**3**). At about this time, too, Sir Cyril and Lady Fox took Sorrell to Ystradfellte to see the *Dervacus* memorial stone, 'Maen Madoc', at which they had done a small excavation and supervised its re-erection for the Ministry of Works. Fox's enthusiasm and the remote scene fired Sorrell's imagination and the result was the dramatic reconstruction, *The Son of Dervacus inspecting his father's monument* (**15**), which he gave to the Foxes as a memento.

All were vivid and, bearing in mind the nature of the evidence, plausible reconstructions and it was hoped that the happy association with the Museum could be continued. Nash-Williams certainly had further ideas but the dislocation of the War interrupted further collaboration. Both Nash-Williams and Sorrell

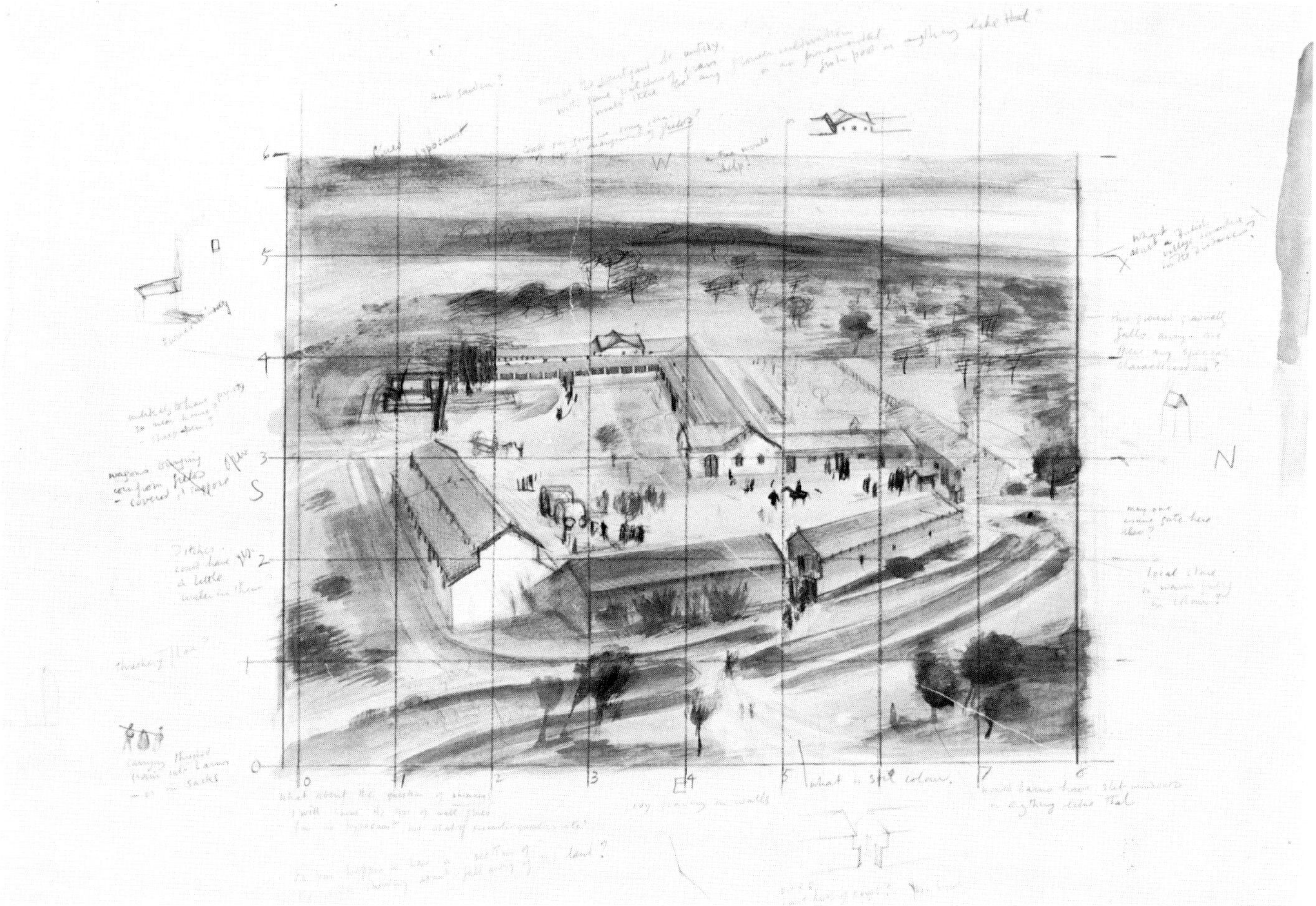
W
S
N
what is stil colour

The Fox Family, 1946

were too heavily taken up with their respective service duties. By now Nash-Williams had been commissioned in the R.A.S.C., and for reasons of safety all Sorrell's pictures had been withdrawn from public display for the duration of the War.

Sorrell's work for the Museum was not resumed until 1948. During the summer of that year Nash-Williams had completed the excavation of the Roman villa at Llantwit-Major and it was generally agreed that this would invite the same treatment that Sorrell had so successfully achieved at Caerleon and Caerwent before the War and which had proved so acceptable to visitors and students in interpreting the results of field-excavations sponsored by the Museum. Again the same technique as of old was followed with visits to the site, preliminary sketches and detailed comments by the expert and the finished picture was completed in 1949 **(8)**.

The last work that Sorrell undertook for the Museum was his graphic reconstructions of the forum and basilica (**11**) and of the Romano-Celtic temple **(12)** at Caerwent in 1955. By then, however, Fox had retired from the Directorship and although a further reconstruction was projected Nash-Williams died after a short illness in December of that year and the close association of artist and expert came to an untimely end.

D. W. Dykes

Alan Sorrell and Ancient Monuments in Wales

Over the years ancient monuments maintained by the state in Wales have been in the care of successively re-named government departments: the Office of Works, the Ministry of Works, the Ministry of Public Building and Works and latterly, the Department of the Environment from which, in April 1978, they were transferred to the Welsh Office.

Until the nineteen-fifties almost the only information provided for the visitor to these monuments was textual, either a notice or a guide book. The ravage of centuries had left the monuments in varying degrees of decay and it was left very much to the ruins themselves to stimulate in the visitor a vision of their 'living' state: to recreate a picture of how the ruins must have looked when in use and what it must have been like to have lived in them.

In the early nineteen-fifties, however, it began to be recognised that graphic illustration was also needed and the Ministry of Works mounted a series of exhibitions to publicise and explain some of the ancient monuments in its care. Displays of photographs and diagrams, with supporting text, were employed to outline the development and function of various types of building, whilst illustrations of parts of other similar buildings that still existed were used for comparison. The exhibitions were shown at various centres around the country and proved to be both successful and popular. In 1956 such an exhibition was in preparation for Hadrian's Wall and here a problem was encountered. In explaining the development of, for example, a medieval castle or abbey, it was possible, without too much difficulty, to find examples of different periods still in existence and thus use one building to explain another. In trying to explain how the Roman wall was built, however, and to show what defensive system was employed, how it was garrisoned and what life was like along it, one was faced with the fact that few Roman remains in this country stand very much higher than foundation

The civil settlement at Housesteads, 1956. One of Sorrell's earliest reconstructions for the Ministry of Works

level. Models of the bridge at Chesters, of a milecastle, a turret and of a section of wall were already in existence and it was decided to add to them three reconstruction drawings of the fort at Housesteads, its civil settlement outside the walls and the supply base at Corbridge.

The Ministry decided to approach Alan Sorrell to undertake these drawings. Sorrell, as has already been mentioned, had collaborated with the Scottish Ancient Monuments Inspectorate on reconstruction drawings of Jarlshof. Moreover, he knew the area of the Wall well, having drawn the Mithraeum at Carrawburgh for the *Illustrated London News* six years earlier with the help of the late Sir Ian Richmond, who was now advising on the proposed exhibition. To Sorrell the sparse uninviting landscape of the Roman frontier was a major attraction in his composition and the three pictures when completed were greatly admired. As in all his other work of this kind they did not claim to be exact reconstructions, but rather to be academically well-founded and based upon the best archaeological and historical evidence available, helped by contemporary illustrations of such forts on Trajan's column in Rome.

Lord Molson, who was Minister of Works at the time, saw the paintings and liked them very much and he urged that further ancient monuments should be considered for similar treatment. There was a certain initial embarrassment at this suggestion since it had for very many years been an established principle that

> *'the Office of Works did not encourage or permit the exhibition of artists' reconstruction drawings of monuments at the monuments in its care: it did not accept such drawings for display either as gifts, or on loan, or on sale-or-return terms or by any other means and it did not include such drawings in any of its official publications.'*

The reason for this very rigid policy was that it was felt that any attempt at reconstruction was bound to be guess work, and that even well informed guess work could never be certainty: thus to sanction any attempt at historical recreation would be to do no more than give official backing to the ideas of one particular artist. The only occasions on which this rule had been relaxed were either at sites not wholly in the Ministry's care or where local schoolchildren had made a model or a drawing of a castle or abbey ruins and this had been accepted not for its reconstruction value but more as an example of the potential influence of ancient monuments in education.

This was a hard policy to overturn and it is a reflection of the considerable esteem in which Sorrell's work was held that a decision was made to commission a series of further reconstruction paintings from him, which were to be reproduced at the monument concerned as well as in the form of postcards for sale. To reinforce this decision it was agreed that a question be put to the Minister of Works in the House of Commons asking

> *'whether he will arrange for drawings of ancient monuments as they might have appeared in use to be displayed at the monuments in his care'.*

The minister's reply to this question, on 23 July 1957 set the seal of approval to a project which was to involve Sorrell for several years to come.

> *'The Ministry of Works are anxious to enable the general public to visualize what ancient monuments looked like in the days when they were in use. Mr. Alan Sorrell has therefore been employed to carry out drawings and has received the advice of the Ministry's architects and archaeologists. There can, of course, be no assurance that the reconstructions are accurate in detail, but it is believed they give a fair impression of what the buildings must have looked like'.*

In preparing his drawings Sorrell followed his well-tried and detailed collaboration with the expert. Altogether, the process involved a good deal of time and effort on both sides, but the end result was a life-like impression that was as near to historical probability as it was possible to achieve.

The first group of reconstructions to be commissioned, after the original drawings of Hadrian's Wall, was of the three major castles of Edward I in North Wales, Conwy **(22)**, Harlech **(24)** and Beaumaris **(25)**. These watercolours were undertaken in 1957 and on all three Sorrell worked closely with Dr. Arnold Taylor, who was then Assistant Chief Inspector of Ancient Monuments and the country's foremost authority on Edwardian castles. The effect of these reconstructions, when completed, was startling. The shining white rendering covering all external wall surfaces, the conical roofs and battlemented parapets and the siege engines standing on their platforms, all presented a surprising new vision of familiar landmarks to the hundreds of thousands of visitors who came to these castles each year. Taylor felt, however, that Caernarfon, as a castle, did not require a reconstruction drawing since it was already, to all intents and purposes, complete; thus it was never included on the list. In the following year Sorrell painted the Bishop's Palace at St. David's **(27)**, again with the help of Taylor: it is interesting to note, when comparing his initial sketch for this with the final version, that in the latter he shifted the viewpoint of the entire painting to the top of the cathedral tower, from where it was felt a better viewpoint of the complex was to be had.

Over the succeeding five years, Sorrell tackled a further twelve Welsh subjects where it was felt that enough evidence survived to make possible a reasonable attempt at reconstruction. In 1962 he undertook his first 'interior' painting for the Ministry in Wales – the Great Hall at Conwy Castle **(23)**. Dr. Taylor recalls persuading Sorrell to use, for the windows in the Hall, the shields of three of Edward I's knights, active in North Wales in the 1280s and to copy, for the wall decoration, the chevron designs surviving from the same period in the castle of Chillon, in Switzerland, and St Faith's Chapel in Westminster Abbey, instead of the more usual painted imitation fine stonework. Writing to Sorrell about this painting, in August 1961, Taylor acknowledged that the subject would be difficult to tackle and said

> *'I am going to make it more difficult still, by wanting this drawing to show the hall as it was originally built, i.e. before the insertion*

Rites at the Temple of Mithras, Carrawburgh, which in their detail would have been enacted at Segontium

A preliminary sketch of the Bishop's Palace at St. David's taken from a different viewpoint from the finished watercolour (**27**)

of the stone arches and the low-pitched roof in the mid 14th century. This is partly because we have no evidence whatever as to how the wall surfaces would have been treated at this time, whereas there are very probable analogies, of which examples survive in colour, of the way they would have been finished when the hall was first built in 1285, and that is what it will be the purpose of the reconstruction to show'.

Another subject very dear to Taylor's heart was an Edwardian walled town. In 1958 he made out a good case for attempting a reconstruction of the town of Conwy, saying that the Ministry had been at pains to maintain the completeness of the walls in the face of modern development and that 'we should do everything in our power to awaken awareness of their unique character to as wide a public as possible'. Sadly, Conwy was never tackled by Sorrell in this way and the only walled town he ever undertook was one of his last three assignments in Wales in 1963, that of Kidwelly **(17)**.

From 1956 until his death in December 1974, Sorrell received commissions for some seventy reconstruction paintings of ancient monuments in the care of the state throughout Britain including the sixteen sites in Wales. Since his death reconstructions have been attempted by other artists but few, so far, have rivalled the verve and vitality of Sorrell's and rarely have such painstaking efforts been made to follow the testimony of the site, to study the source material in depth or to seek out evidence by analogy from elsewhere.

Peter Humphries

Catalogue

1 **Tinkinswood, St. Nicholas, South Glamorgan.**
Reconstruction of a burial scene at the neolithic chambered tomb

Signed, 1940. 50.5 x 66 cm. National Museum of Wales

In 1940 Alan Sorrell undertook three reconstruction paintings of prehistoric sites in South Wales for the National Museum. On all of them he worked in close collaboration with Sir Cyril Fox. The burial chamber at Tinkinswood is one of a group of neolithic monuments of about the fourth millennium B.C. similar to the ones found on the Cotswolds and around the Severn estuary. They were erected for the multiple burial of members of the same family or community; their bones being deposited in a chamber constructed of very large stone slabs which was set in the end of a long cairn.

Tinkinswood was excavated in 1914 by John Ward, first Keeper of Archaeology at the National Museum (see *Archaeologia Cambrensis* 1915, 253–320; 1916, 259–94). It was found to contain the fragmentary remains of over 50 individuals, together with flint and pottery grave goods, now in the National Museum. The painting depicts the ceremony which might have accompanied an interment in the tomb.

2 Pond Cairn, Coity, Mid Glamorgan. A Bronze Age burial: the last rites

Signed, 1940. 43 x 66 cm. National Museum of Wales

Sir Cyril Fox excavated Pond Cairn in 1937 in advance of its destruction by the War Office (see *Archaeologia* 1937, 129–80). The results of that excavation pointed to the performance of an elaborate, dramatic and prolonged ritual at the mound, which was the burial place of a person of some importance during the Early Bronze Age, *c.* 2000 B.C. His cremated bones, which had first been placed in an urn within a pit and then covered with charcoal and clay, were sealed under a vertical- sided mound. This had been surrounded by a ring of stones and then sprinkled with wood ash. Finally, the stone ring had been broken through to dig a pit; this had been fired and an offering made of corn sheaves. The painting is an attempt to show the final stages of that ritual.

3 Llanmelin, Gwent. Reconstruction of the main entrance of the Iron Age hillfort

Signed, 1940. 55.5 x 55.5 cm. National Museum of Wales

Llanmelin Wood Camp lies about a mile to the north west of Caerwent. Defended by ramparts and ditches, such hillforts are common throughout most of Britain and they served both for occasional communal defence and as permanent settlements. That at Llanmelin was occupied by the Silures, and was excavated by Dr. V. E. Nash-Williams in the early 1930s (see *Archaeologia Cambrensis* 1933, 237-346). It covers three acres, enclosed mainly by twin banks and ditches and, to judge by the excavated pottery, would have been built around 250 B.C. The entrance was remodelled in about 50 B.C. and the fort was occupied towards the Roman conquest. Sorrell's painting shows an imaginary scene at the entrance to the hillfort before its later remodelling.

4 Caerleon, Gwent. A bird's eye view of the Roman fortress

Signed, 1939. 66 x 93.5 cm. National Museum of Wales

Sorrell painted three reconstructions of the Roman legionary fortress at Caerleon during 1939. He worked on these, as on those of the other major Roman site at Caerleon, in close consultation with Nash-Williams. Caerleon was the headquarters of the 2nd Augustan legion and was the chief military base for the control of South Wales. It was built *c.*A.D.75, about the time of the final pacification of the country, and enclosed some 50 acres. The original defences of earth and timber were rebuilt in stone during the second century and the fortress contained accommodation for 5-6,000 heavily armed infantry and their officers, together with granaries, baths and a hospital. Outside the walls was an amphitheatre, a parade ground and a civil settlement (growth of which was stunted, probably, by the existence near-by of Caerwent), all of which may be seen in this bird's eye view.

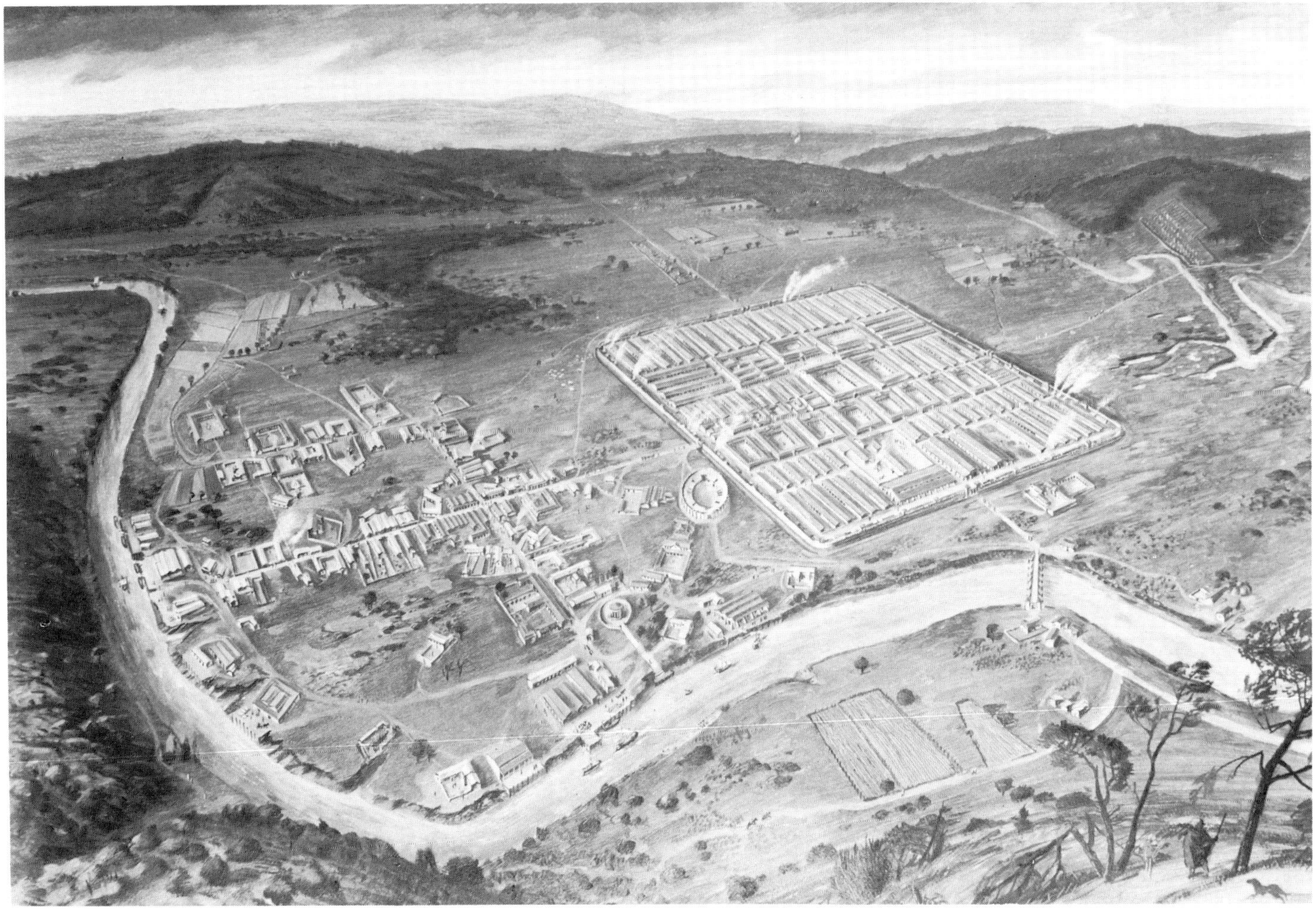

5 **Caerleon, Gwent. The Roman amphitheatre with the fortress in the background**

Signed, 1939. 43 x 55.5 cm. National Museum of Wales

Two main areas of the Roman fortress at Caerleon have been laid out and opened to the public. One is the west corner of the fortress (the subject of the following painting) and the other is the amphitheatre. It was a large oval structure, open to the sky, with an arena roughly 57 x 42 m. hollowed out of the ground. Earthen banks, which supported the timber seating, were retained by an encircling buttressed wall of masonry, but the superstructure is now thought to have been wholly of timber above the present level of the banks, not stone, as shown here. The amphitheatre was built in about A.D.80, much the same time as the Colosseum in Rome. It has been estimated that its seating capacity must have been about 6,000, which would have accommodated the entire legion.

6 **Caerleon, Gwent. Reconstruction of barracks and other buildings in the west corner of the Roman fortress**

Signed, 1939. 43 x 55.5 cm. National Museum of Wales

This reconstruction shows the one area of the barracks in Prysg Field now laid out and on view to the public. Three of the many blocks of barracks can be seen within the fortress walls. Each block housed a century of 80 men, together with its centurion and his staff. The rampart is shown with its outer ditch, its masonry wall and inner earth bank and sentry turrets at intervals along it. Beneath the tiled lean-to roof, on the inner side of the rampart, were workshops and stores with a latrine next to them; while along the further edge of the rampart, towards the top of the picture, were ovens and cookhouses. Part of the civil settlement outside the fortress is shown in the background.

7 Segontium Roman Fort, Gwynedd. View from the south as it might have appeared in the third century A.D.

Signed, 1962. 39 x 54.5 cm. Welsh Office

Segontium is the only major Roman site in North Wales on display to the public. The fort was built in about A.D. 78 when the Roman army subdued this part of Wales. It was an important bastion of imperial power in the west and, for the greater part of three centuries, was garrisoned by a cohort of auxiliary troops (differing from legionaries in that they were not Roman citizens, but drafted in from other parts of the empire). The fort at Segontium was originally built of earth and timber, but the defences and internal buildings were replaced in stone after A.D. 150. Sorrell's bird's eye view shows the fort as it might have looked some time after this rebuilding.

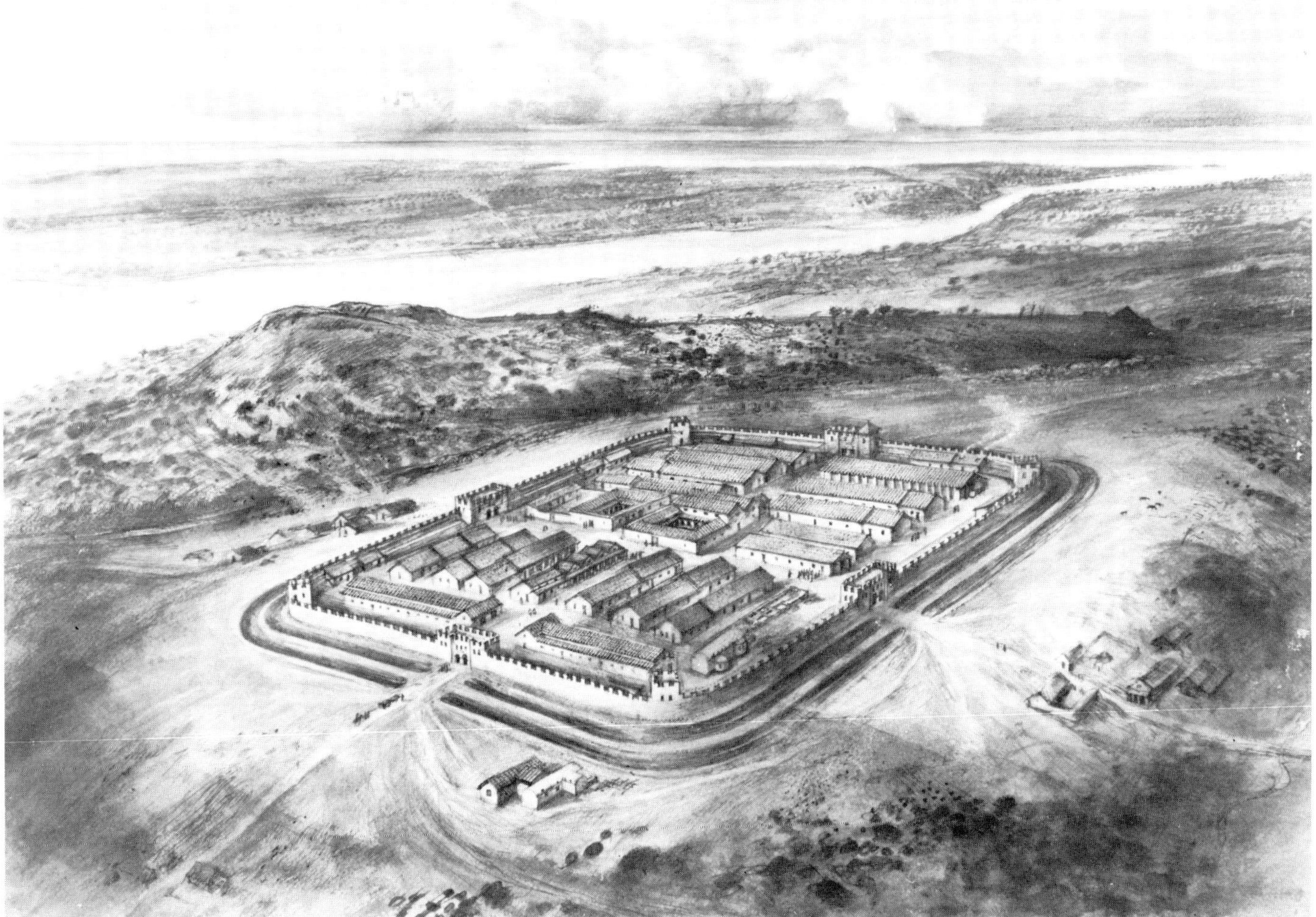

8 Llantwit Major, South Glamorgan. Reconstruction of the Roman villa, as it might have appeared in the fourth century A.D.

Signed, 1949. 61 x 76.5 cm. National Museum of Wales

This reconstruction was painted by Sorrell the year after the final season of excavation at the site by Nash-Williams (see *Archaeologia Cambrensis* 1952–3, 89–163). Those excavations had revealed the plan of a villa of quite elaborate type, which was the largest in this part of South Wales. Several ranges of buildings lay around an L shaped courtyard and the area was protected with encircling banks and ditches. The accommodation comprised living rooms, sleeping quarters, a bath block and workshops, together with other subsidiary buildings, barns and stables. Nash-Williams formed the opinion that the whole complex was built *c.* A.D. 150, reached its zenith during the third century and then underwent a period of decline. Evidence of more recent excavations, however, has shown that the villa, as Sorrell has drawn it, did not come into existence until the late third or fourth century A.D. and had a stone, not a tiled roof.

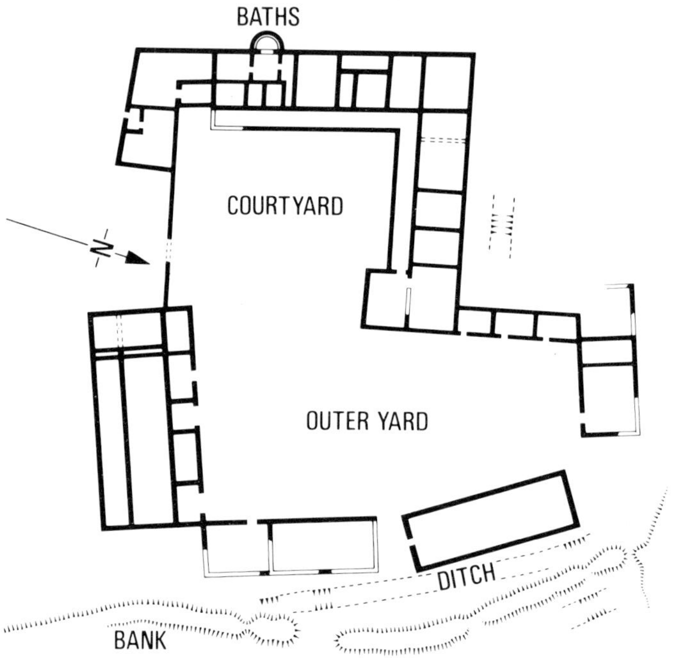

9 Caerwent, Gwent. A bird's eye view of the Roman town

Signed, 1937.   70 x 93.5 cm.   National Museum of Wales

This was the earliest picture undertaken by Sorrell for the Museum and was the first of several he was to paint of the Roman town of Caerwent. Like his later painting of Caerleon (**4**), it is a general view showing the entire walled town of 44 acres, its streets, its defences and its main public buildings.
Caerwent was established in about A.D. 75, and became the new market town and administrative centre of the Silures. It had the customary Roman rectangular layout on a grid plan and was divided into 20 blocks or *insulae* by its intersecting streets. The chief public buildings of forum, basilica and baths occupied the centre of the town, with houses and shops in the remainder.

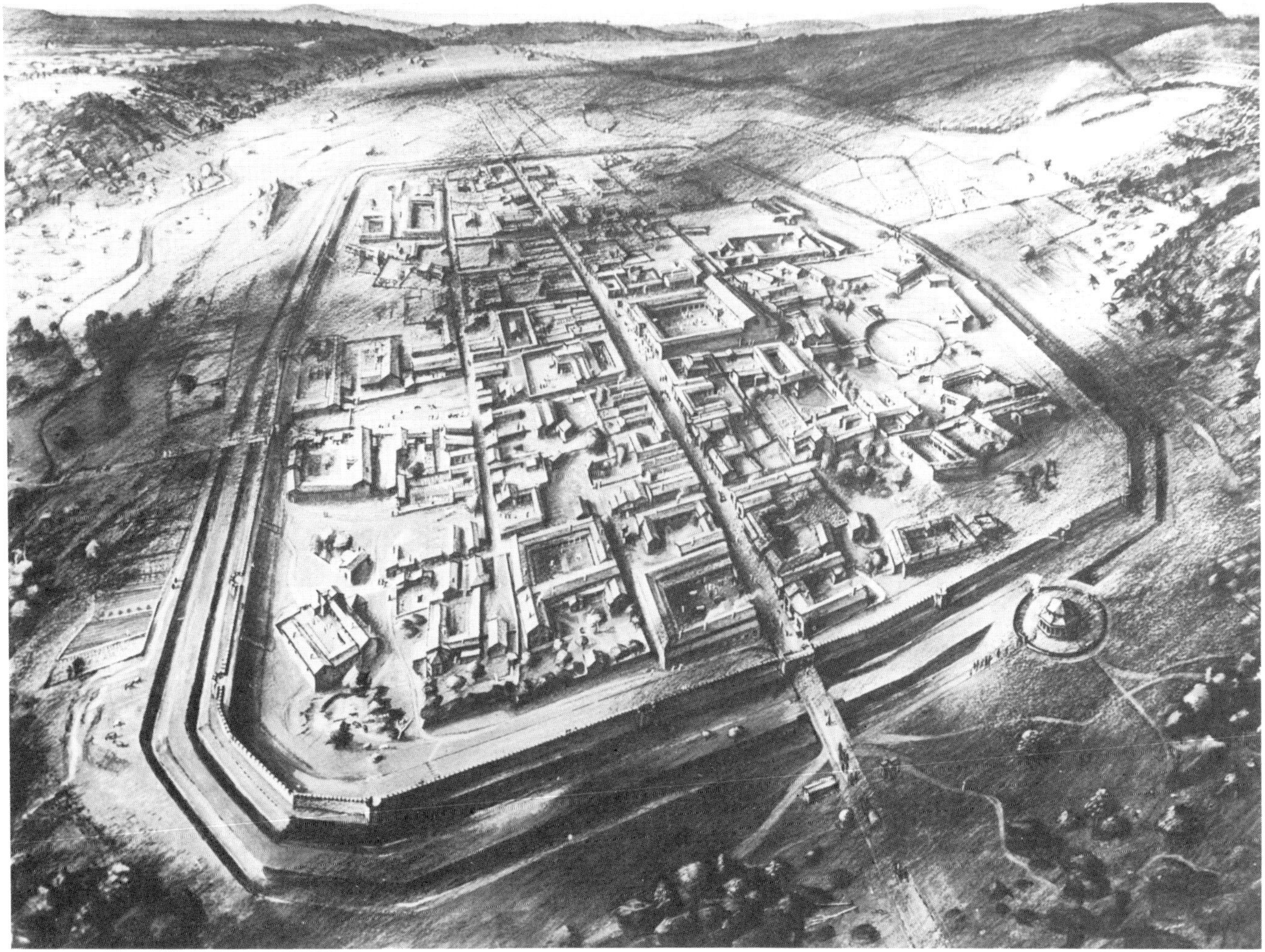

10 Caerwent, Gwent. A reconstruction of Roman shops and houses in the second century based on the evidence of excavations. In the foreground is the main street: on the right is the basilica or town hall

Signed, 1958. 41 x 57.5 cm. Welsh Office

This is one of two reconstructions of Roman sites in Wales painted by Sorrell for the then Ministry of Works. It shows the area at Pound Lane, Caerwent, which was excavated between 1947 and 1955 and is now laid out and opened to public view. Those excavations showed that there had been shops and houses on the site throughout the Roman period, various modifications having been carried out at several stages. This painting shows it as it might have looked in its later period. The street is lined by a colonnaded frontage and behind this is a fairly typical courtyard house; in its earlier phase, this courtyard house had been two narrow dwellings with shops fronting the street. In the background to the right is the basilica of the Roman town.

11 Caerwent, Gwent. Reconstruction of the forum and basilica – market place and town hall – in the centre of the Roman town

Signed, 1955. 33 x 91.5 cm. National Museum of Wales

This is one of only three paintings executed by Sorrell for the Museum after the War and shows the two chief public buildings in the Roman town. The forum was enclosed on three sides by colonnades, from which opened shops and offices. The basilica, forming the fourth side of the square, was approached from the forum up a flight of steps and consisted of a nave and two aisles, with a further range of rooms opening off the north aisle. More recent research suggests that the forum front of the basilica was colonnaded, and has since disproved several points of detail in this painting (as in some of Sorrell's other Roman reconstructions), but nonetheless, it portrays well enough the general atmosphere and layout of this area.

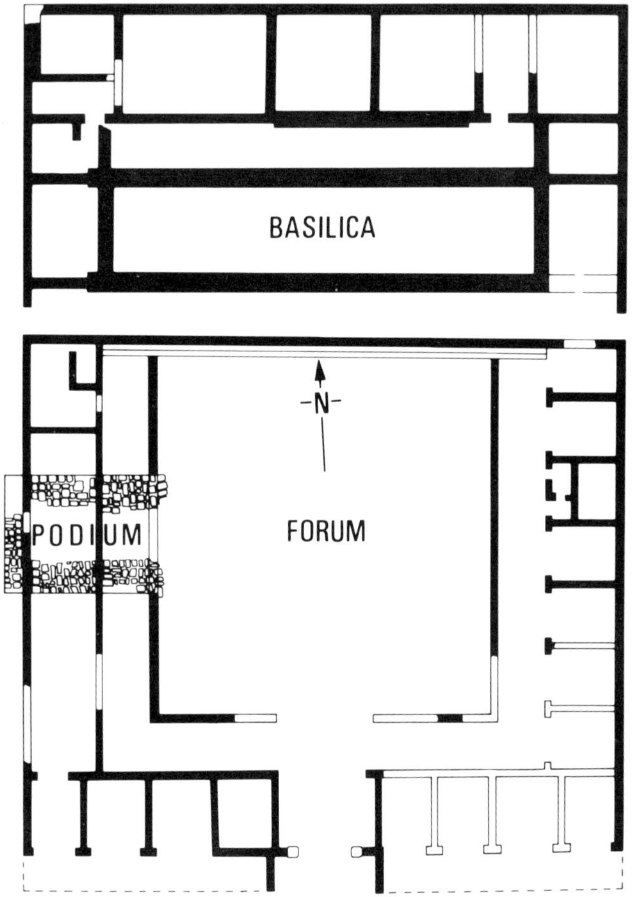

12 Caerwent, Gwent. Reconstruction of the Romano-Celtic temple: on the left is the forum and basilica

Signed, 1955. 70 x 91.5 cm. National Museum of Wales

The area of the temple, near the forum at Caerwent, has now been laid out and is on view to the public. The site was excavated by T. Ashby, A. Hudd and F. King in 1908 (See *Archaeologia* 1910, 1–20) and proved to be a Romano-Celtic temple of normal layout, with an apse projecting from its north side across the rear portico. Behind the temple was a house, set in its own courtyard, with an entrance portico opening from the street to the west. The street fronting the temple complex, in the foreground of Sorrell's reconstruction, was lined by shops with living accommodation at their rear.

13 Caerwent, Gwent. Imaginative reconstruction of a raid on the south west corner of the Roman town

Signed, 1938. 45 x 65 cm. National Museum of Wales

The houses in the south west corner of Caerwent were excavated by A. T. Martin and T. Ashby in 1899 and 1900 (See *Archaeologia* 1901, 295–316). Two houses were found to have existed in this area: their plans showed considerable Mediterranean influence – buildings being ranged around all four sides of a central colonnaded courtyard, which in Italy was designed to give shade, though in this country would have been more useful as protection from inclement weather. From their size, they must have been occupied by men of some importance in the Roman town. The house in the foreground has an attached lean-to latrine block, flushed by collected rainwater and beyond it, inside the paling fence, is the furnace house for the hypocaust heating system.

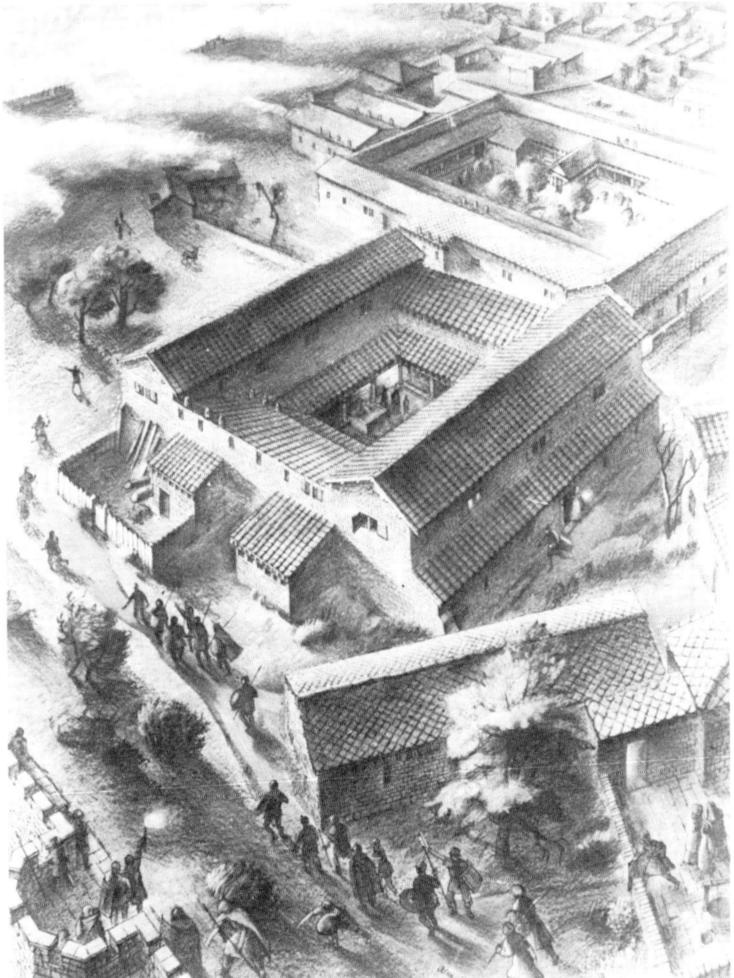

14 Caerwent, Gwent. Reconstruction of the supposed post Roman church

Signed, 1938. 56 x 43 cm. National Museum of Wales

The Roman baths at Caerwent were excavated by Nash-Williams in 1923. Those excavations showed the remains of another small building in the north-western angle of the baths which not only overlay their ruined colonnade, but whose foundations were somewhat higher and had thus been built some considerable time after the destruction of the baths. From its size and orientation, Nash-Williams suggested that this building was a small Christian church of early post-Roman date (See *Archaeologia* 1930, 253–6). Sorrell's reconstruction shows this small building restored as a church, with crosses at its gable ends. It is set amongst the by now half ruined buildings of the Roman town. More recent reappraisal of the evidence, however, suggests that this building is not of sub-Roman date, but is in fact the remains of a post-medieval cottage.

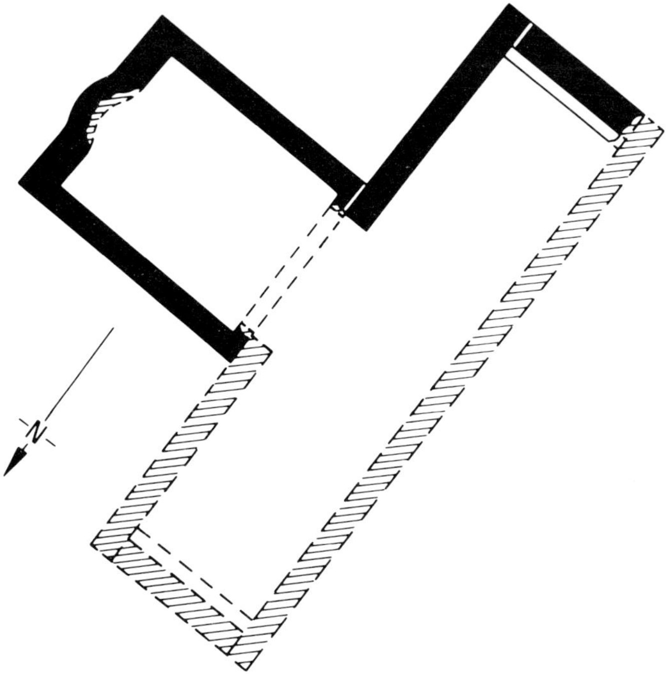

15 Maen Madoc, Ystradfellte, Powys: the son of Dervacus inspects his father's monument

Signed, 1940. 26.5 x 37.5 cm.   Collection of Lady Fox

The early fifth century inscribed grave stone to Dervacus, son of Justus, traditionally known as 'Maen Madoc', stands on a remote site beside the Roman road between the forts at Neath and Brecon. Its re-erection in 1940 under the supervision of Sir Cyril and Lady Fox was the occasion for this picture which Sorrell gave to the Foxes as a memento. Fox's report pointed to the location of the stone as indicating the continuation into the Dark Ages of the Roman practice of burying their dead beside highways, though no grave was found in this instance. Of Sorrell's reconstruction he writes that it is 'intended to suggest in the dress and bearing of the "son of Dervacus" the same continuity of Roman tradition as does the name Justus, the Roman script and language, and the position of the memorial. The mountain in the left background is Fan Nedd'. (*Archaeologia Cambrensis* 1940, 215.)

16 Carreg Cennen Castle, Dyfed. As it might have appeared before it was dismantled in 1462

Signed, 1960. 41 x 57.5 cm. Welsh Office

Carreg Cennen, the ancient centre and stronghold of the commote of Is-Cennen, lies in the foothills of the Black Mountains, south-east of Llandeilo, Dyfed. It is one of a group of castles in south-west Wales which in the twelfth and thirteenth centuries frequently changed hands between Welsh and English. The present building is mainly English work of the late thirteenth–early fourteenth century. It is perched spectacularly on a limestone crag, its south curtain wall hugging the edge of a cliff 90 m. above the river Cennen. Sorrell's painting views it from the north east, and shows the relatively slight defences of the outer ward, inside which the ramped barbican, elaborately defended by gates and bridges, offers the only access to the massively walled inner ward.

17 Kidwelly Castle, Dyfed. The town and castle, as it might have appeared towards the middle of the fifteenth century

Signed, 1963. 41 x 57 cm. Welsh Office

Kidwelly, like many other castles in West Wales, was originally a Welsh stronghold. The present castle is of late thirteenth–early fourteenth century date and consists of a square inner ward with a tower at each corner, standing on a steep scarp above the river, and encircled on the landward side by a semi-circular outer ward. Adjoining the castle was a fortified borough, which Sorrell has shown in its entirety, which makes this picture unique among his reconstructions. Apart from the gatehouse, little remains of this town and its defences, though its street plan is traceable.

18 Castell-y-Bere, Gwynedd. As it might have appeared before its destruction at the end of the thirteenth century

Signed, 1961. 38,5 x 54.5 cm. Welsh Office

Castell-y-Bere occupies a lonely and spectacular position a little to the south of Cader Idris. It was one of three original Welsh castles – Cricieth and Dolwyddelan are the others – captured and partly rebuilt by Edward I after the death of Llywelyn ap Gruffydd in 1282. The castle was first founded by Llywelyn ab Iorwerth (Llywelyn the Great) in 1221. Edward's forces captured it by siege on 25 April 1283 and, after the departure of the army, five masons and five carpenters remained behind to carry out various works. Exactly what these works were and what became of the castle after it was retaken in the Welsh revolt of 1294 is not known with certainty, but it seems never again to have played any very active part in Welsh affairs. (See *Archaeologia Cambrensis* 1974, 78–112.)

Alan Sorrell

19 Cricieth Castle, Gwynedd. As it might have appeared at the end of the thirteenth century

Signed, 1961. 38.5 x 54.4 cm. Welsh Office

Cricieth, like Castell-y-Bere (**18**) was captured and partly rebuilt by Edward I in the Welsh war of 1282–3. The castle is first mentioned in 1239, and was probably founded by Llywelyn the Great. From 1259 it was in the possession of his grandson, Llywelyn ap Gruffydd, and was still held by him at his death in December 1282. No details of its taking by Edward's forces are known, but it was in English hands by 14 March 1283. Later it withstood the rising under Madog in 1294–5, but in the turbulent period around 1400, during the uprising of Owain Glyndwr, it was burned and left derelict. Sorrell's painting shows it as it might have looked after the rebuilding of Edward I; a trébuchet, or engine for hurling missiles by means of a counterpoised weight, is shown on the Engine Tower in the foreground of the picture.

20 **Denbigh Castle, Clwyd. Showing the gatehouse as it might have appeared when complete**

Signed, 1961. 39 x 55 cm. Welsh Office

Denbigh was one of five lordship castles built during the second Welsh war of Edward I. These castles were not built and funded directly by the crown, but by English lords loyal to the king, in the furtherence of royal policy. Denbigh had previously been the site of a stronghold of the Welsh princes, but nothing of this foundation now remains. On 16 October 1282 the lordship was granted to Henry de Lacy, Earl of Lincoln, and the present castle was undoubtedly begun within a few days, for the king and de Lacy were both present to watch building operations during the last ten days of that month, and some royal resources were used to help with initial building costs. Also present in the early months was the king's master mason, James of St. George, who was doubtless responsible for the design of Denbigh's elaborate triple towered gatehouse, shown here in detail in Sorrell's reconstruction.

21 Rhuddlan Castle, Clwyd. As it might have appeared towards the end of the thirteenth century

Signed, 1963. 38.5 x 54.5 cm. Welsh Office

Rhuddlan was one of the major castles of Edward I's campaign in Wales of 1276–7. It was built close to the earlier Norman motte and bailey castle of 1073, whose earth mound may still be seen today, although it is outside the area included in Sorrell's reconstruction. Edward I's castle had a diamond shaped inner ward with two opposing twin towered gatehouses, surrounded by a much lower outer wall which, on the south west, extended to the river to form a protected dock for shipping. Edward's strategy for the conquest of Gwynedd relied heavily upon maritime communication and resources, and before castle building could begin at Rhuddlan about three miles of the river course of the Clwyd had first to be widened to make it navigable to sea-going shipping. In this reconstruction the castle is viewed from the south west, across the river, with the dock visible in the foreground.

22 Conwy Castle, Gwynedd. As it is believed it would have appeared at the time of its completion about the year 1290

Signed, 1957. 39 x 55 cm. Welsh Office

The castle of Conwy, together with those of Harlech (**24**) and Beaumaris (**25**) was among the first group of reconstructions formally commissioned from Sorrell by the Ministry of Works after his three trial drawings of Hadrian's Wall in 1956. Conwy was one of the three major castles of King Edward I's second and final campaign in North Wales of 1282–3. Built where the Gyffin stream runs into the estuary of the Conwy, it lay directly on the main route across North Wales to the Welsh heartland of Gwynedd. Its rocky siting determined its linear plan of two conjoined rectangular wards, with four pairs of circular towers. As at Caernarfon, the castle formed the main stronghold of a fortified town whose medieval street plan and enclosing wall may still be seen to this day: in Sorrell's picture the town wall can be seen running off to the left. The battlemented parapets, conical roofs and the white rendering of the castle, make a striking contrast to the dark stone walls of the roofless ruin that remains today.

ALAN SORRELL 57

23 Conwy Castle, Gwynedd. The great hall as it might have appeared when first built c. 1285

Signed, 1962. 39 x 55 cm. Welsh Office

The great hall of Conwy now stands a gutted shell, roofless, floorless and open to the elements. The main hall stood above a cellar and, when first built, it had a timber roof as shown in the reconstruction, the stone arched roof whose remains can be seen today being a later modification of 1346–7. The great hall was the main place of assembly in a medieval castle where formal business was transacted, meals taken and guests received and entertained. At one end was a raised dais, on which the nobility ate at 'high table', while at the opposite end there was usually a carved timber screen concealing the service rooms. This reconstruction shows a meal in progress, viewed towards the dais end of the hall. It shows the details of the roof, the windows and the fireplace and also the type of painted decoration which might once have covered the plastered walls. The shields of three of Edward I's knights who were active in North Wales in the 1280s were incorporated in the windows and the chevron pattern decoration adopted for the walls was copied from surviving work of the same period in the Castle of Chillon and in St. Faith's Chapel in Westminster Abbey.

24 Harlech castle, Gwynedd. As it is believed it would have appeared at the time of its completion about the year 1290

Signed, 1957. 39 x 55 cm. Welsh Office

Harlech is the third of the great new castles of Edward I begun in 1283, but, unlike Conwy and Caernarfon, it had no walled town attached. It is seen here from the well-known viewpoint on the rock to the south. Work upon it began at the end of April 1283 and by 1290 the castle stood complete after an expediture of some 8,000 pounds (equivalent at today's values to between four and five million pounds). Today the castle is landlocked, the sea having receded well over half a mile since the Middle Ages, when the rock probably rose straight out of the sea, as Sorrell had depicted it. The castle might thus have been supplied entirely by ship through its sea gate which led to a fortified way up the rock. In the painting the seaward side is defended by two artillery engines standing on specially constructed platforms.

25 Beaumaris Castle, Anglesey. The castle, begun in 1295 and left unfinished in 1323, as it might have appeared if the architect's conception had been carried to completion

Signed, 1957. 39 x 55 cm. Welsh Office

Beaumaris was the most perfect example of 'concentric castle' planning, in which the multiplication of lines of defence had led to the building of what are in effect two castles, one inside the other. It was the last of the great series of castles in North Wales designed for Edward I by his military architect Master James of St. George. It was begun in 1295 after a revolt in North Wales, but was never completed. Building went on continuously until 1298, after which only minimal work was carried out. Sorrell's conjectural painting shows it as there is good reason to believe it would have looked if it had been completed, taking into account the surviving architectural evidence and that of other castles of the series.

26 Raglan Castle, Gwent. The castle as it might have appeared at the time of King Charles I's visit to Raglan in 1645

Signed, 1959. 41 x 57.5 cm. Welsh Office

The fifteenth century castle of Raglan was one of the last to be built in Wales. Though it replaced an earlier castle, the style of its architecture is as much that of a grand fortified residence as of a purely military structure. It was begun *c.* 1435 by Sir William ap Thomas, later additions being made by his heirs the Herbert family during the latter part of that century and the early part of the next. In plan, the castle consists of a series of buildings ranged around two courtyards, with a central dividing hall-block between them. At the south, and outside the main castle area, is an entirely separate and self-contained tower, the 'Yellow Tower of Gwent', probably on the site of the original motte. This tower may be seen on the left in Sorrell's reconstruction: it was surrounded by a moat and a low fortified wall, and its lowest level was provided with gunports.

27 St. David's Dyfed. The Bishop's Palace, as it might have appeared from the tower of the Cathedral in c.1530

Signed, 1958. 41 x 57 cm. Welsh Office

Built mainly between 1280 and 1350, the Bishop's Palace at St. David's stands within the Cathedral Close, among a group of buildings unique in Wales. These embody an unbroken Christian tradition extending back to the sixth century, though nothing now remains of the monastic foundation of St. David near Whitesands Bay, or of the Celtic monastery on the Cathedral site, which grew out of it. The Bishop's Palace as it stands now, consists of three ranges of buildings around a square courtyard: the accommodation comprised a private wing for the bishop, as well as formal, domestic and storage areas. The present appearance of the Palace owes much to the work of Bishop Henry Gower, 1327–47, who was responsible for building the Great Hall, seen at the left in Sorrell's reconstruction, and for adding the arcaded parapets around the roofs, which give the whole complex a unified and pleasing appearance. After the Reformation the Palace fell on evil days and was allowed to fall into decay.

28 Tintern Abbey, Gwent. The Abbey as it might have appeared before the dissolution of the monasteries

Signed, 1959. 39 x 55 cm. Welsh Office

Tintern Abbey was founded in 1131 for monks of the Cistercian Order, which placed great emphasis on simplicity of living and manual labour as being inseparable from the religious vocation. It was more successful in Wales than any other Order, thirteen monasteries, all in remote sites, being established between 1131 and 1226. The present buildings at Tintern are mostly of the thirteenth century, the rebuilt Abbey Church (1270–1307) owing much to the munificence of Roger Bigod, Earl of Norfolk and Lord of Chepstow. It rightly dominates Sorrell's picture, with the domestic buildings of the Abbey grouped round the cloister to the left and with the roofs and chimneys of the Infirmary and Abbot's lodging just visible behind. The long range to the left of the Church housed the lay-brothers, who worked the Abbey lands. In the foreground are workshops and a mill, but the latter is now known not to have occupied this position.

29 Valle Crucis Abbey, Clwyd. The interior of the abbey church: the monks are shown entering the church from their dormitory at dawn

Signed, 1963. 41 x 57 cm. Welsh Office

Valle Crucis, founded in 1201, was another abbey of the Cistercian Order and, like Tintern, it was sited in a remote river valley, where it depended for survival largely on its agricultural and pastoral activities. Accommodation arrangements in medieval abbeys tended to follow a broadly similar plan with domestic buildings grouped around three sides of a cloister attached to the abbey church. The monks slept in a communal dormitory on the first floor of the east range, from where a 'night stair' gave direct access to the church for attendance at the night-time offices. In Sorrell's reconstruction the monks are shown in procession descending into the Monks' Choir to celebrate an early morning office.

Books illustrated by Alan Sorrell

In the nineteen-sixties and seventies Alan Sorrell illustrated or himself wrote and illustrated a number of archaeological and historical books aimed chiefly at the youngster, the student or the general reader. Some of these works have now run into several editions and the dates given below are of the first imprint.

Sorrell also illustrated the Revised Standard Version of the *Bible*, published by William Collins Sons and Co. Limited for the United Society for Christian Literature (Lutterworth Press).

Published by Lutterworth Press:

Roman Britain with Aileen Fox	1961
Saxon England with John Hamilton	1964
Norman Britain with Henry Loyn	1966
Prehistoric Britain with Barbara Green	1968
Imperial Rome with Anthony Birley	1970
Medieval Britain with Henry Loyn (Completed by Richard Sorrell)	1975

Published by B. T. Batsford Limited:

Living History	1965
Roman London	1969
British Castles	1973
Roman Towns in Britain	1977

Published by Oxford University Press:

Stories from Livy by R. M. Ogilvie	1970

Published by Michael Joseph

Age by Age by Ronald Jessup	1967

Published by Longmans Young Books Limited

Nubia – A Drowning Land by Margaret Drower	1970

To be published by B. T. Batsford Limited in 1981:
Reconstructing the Past edited by Mark Sorrell

Designed by Penknife
Typeset by Garland Graphics
Printed by South Western Printers